Mind the H

Memories of Winson Green

Gloria Jenkins

**BREWIN
BOOKS**

First published by Brewin Books Ltd
in December 1999

ISBN 1 85858 159 1

British Library Cataloguing in Publication Data
A Catalogue record for this book is available from the British
Library

ERRATUM

Page 5: Should read
"in the 1880's" not in the 1980's
and
"evicted in the early 1900's" not 1990's.

Typeset in Baskerville and
Made and Printed by
Heron Press, Kings Norton

Preface

Sayings said by our parents to their children on their growing up tends to stay with them throughout life.

Prior to the 1940s, before the cars encroached our roads, which were looked on as an intruder into what had been our play area.

"Mind the 'orse road" on going out to play.

"Mind the 'orse road" on going to school.

"Mind the 'orse road" on going to the shops.

"Mind the 'orse road". The sound of our parents voices many years on, still ringing in our ears.

With that memory as you open the pages of my book, I hope you can visualise a childhood memory of playtime just minding the 'orses!

Winson Green

Let me take you down memory lane of life in the 1920s and 1930s. Where the pavements were not paved with gold but with hard working people.

A place that can only be described as a centre with streets leading off to Smethwick, Ladywood, Handsworth and Edgbaston. Hearing the historian Dr. Carl Chinn, on our local radio talking about Birmingham made me want to write my memories of life living in Winson Green.

Foreword
Dr. Carl Chinn

For too many people, the past is an unknown continent which can be seen only from afar and which inspires a little concern about what dangers may lurk beyond its shores.

But the past should never be regarded in this way. It is not a foreign place which should be shied away from. It is as much a part of our present as it will be our future and it needs to be grasped in a familiar and knowing way. For without a past that we can catch hold of and appreciate we can have neither a present nor a future.

This crucial understanding is emphasised through the intuitive and evocative words of Gloria Jenkins. In *Mind the Horse Road*, she has successfully brought to the fore not only her childhood and youth in the 1920s and 1930s but also the lives of the folk amongst whom she lived in Winson Green. Her tale is neither one of desperate poverty nor of great wealth. It is a story of the hardships and happinesses which were endured and enjoyed by so many working-class people. Gloria Jenkins captures the treat of sweets, the joys of friendship, the closeness of family, the vitality of the Bull Ring, the dominating presence of the black range, her favourite games and so much more. This is a book with which many people will identify, for in bringing to us aspects of her life, Gloria Jenkins has struck chords with the lives of so many others.

The Beginning

The first ten years of my childhood from 1926-1937, were spent living in Winson Green. Although being referred to as the bad old days of the 1930s, I can recall times of happiness and smiles at the antics us kids got up to, while our parents were obviously busy making the housekeeping money go as far as possible.

I decided to delve into the family history. My Grandfather, Charles Joseph Wise, met and married Thurza Hughes at St. Marks Church, Ladywood on 2nd August 1897. They lived at 2/38, Springfield Street, Ladywood. They had two daughters May and Thurza and two sons Charles and Harry. Charles was eventually to be my father. This was quite a revelation to discover dad was born in Ladywood. In my research I found the area, unfortunately only the street names survived. The back-to-back houses and courtyards had all gone.

With a growing family they needed a larger house, and moved to 128, Wellington Street, Winson Green. My father, after the First World War, volunteered to serve five years in the Army. He was posted to the Tank Corps. Some of his service was spent in India, where he trained as a cook, although I cannot recall him trying out his culinary talents on the family. He was also quite clever at boxing for his regiment. I can believe that after suffering a few bruises playfully boxing with him!

Eventually he left India to return to England and was stationed at Bovington Camp, Dorset. Nearby was the sea-side town of Swanage. It was on one of his visits to Swanage that he met a girl named Gertrude and fell in love, they got married in the town's local church.

He had now completed his Army service, but as there was little prospect of getting work, they decided to come back to Winson

Mum & Dad on their Wedding Day.
1925, Swanage, Dorset.

Green in his home town of Birmingham.

They lived with his mother, father, brother Harry and his sisters May and Thurza. Gran's house was one of the larger type of terraced house, with a double front, the door leading into the parlour known as the best room only used on special occasions. A step led you into the living room, the coal fire giving a warm glow high-lighting the marble fire surround. Above an oak over-mantel with shelves full of knick knacks. In the centre of the room stood a large wooden table covered with a red velour cloth adorned with tassels hanging down the sides. Another door led into a small passage with access to the yard and entry. Stepping up into the kitchen a large black range with an oven seemed to take over the kitchen. Most of the baking was done in the oven to save on gas. Up the corner was the brick built wash boiler fitted with a heavy wooden lid. Underneath was a place for the coal to be put for lighting to heat the water. This was done religiously every Monday morning. The house downstairs was lit by gas light using a very flimsy like mantle. Up the steep lino covered stairs was a long landing with four bedrooms leading off. Candle or paraffin lamps were used for lighting.

I was their first born daughter weighing 7lbs and named Gloria Irene on July 13th 1926. Eighteen months later my brother Gerald was born on 5th February 1928. He weighed over nine pounds. I was christened at Bishop Latimers Church on August 1st 1926. My brother was also christened there in 1928.

The church was situated in Handsworth New Road, Winson Green.

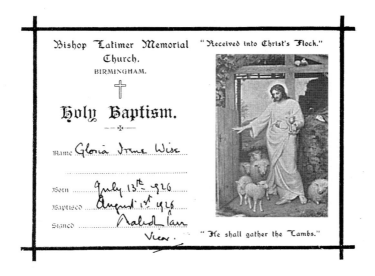

The Dispensary

My first memory I can recall was mum taking us to the local dispensary. A large coloured rocking horse for children to have a ride whilst waiting to be seen by the nurse, was a welcome distraction. When it became our turn to be seen, inevitably the same remarks would be said to mum, "Gloria is rather underweight!" Another bottle of cod liver oil and malt to take home. I could not stand the stuff, even now I shudder when I imagine a spoonful sliding down my throat. There was no problem with

Gerald and myself taken at "Jeromes"
Birmingham City Centre 1928.

my brothers weight, but then he did weigh two pounds heavier when he was born.

Occasionally the dispensary arranged a charabanc to take the children out on a day-trip. We would be given a paper bag with an assortment of sweets in, our mothers would have put some sandwiches up for us on our special day-out.

There weren't many cars about in the 1920s or the early 1930s. We did have to watch for the "Tizer" lorry going back to their factory at the bottom end of Wellington Street. Unfortunately my brother Gerald was knocked down by the driver of a "Tizer" lorry. He brought him over to mum and gave him an orange, I don't know what my mum thought! But luckily he wasn't badly hurt.

Black Patch Park at the bottom of Wellington Street, was a favourite place for us kids to play. We always made for the swings, especially the one called the spider so named because of the cone shape and the bars arranged in a web-like fashion. We would sit on the wooden slats and be pushed round by a friend before they quickly jumped on. Great fun until the boys decided to push it backwards and forwards against the centre pole, causing us to bounce up and down resulting in a few bruised backsides! Seesaws and roundabouts were also there. A running ditch separated the park from the grass area. To get there you needed to go out of the gate into the road over the ditch and through another gate. This is where we played rounders or French cricket.

In the 1980s there was a gypsy encampment in the park, after being there for many years, they were finally evicted in the early 1990s. Not before putting up a terrific fight against the officers sent to move them on.

Opposite Black Patch Park lived my Grandmother's sister aunt Liza. Most days she would come up to our house. She was a very down to earth person, a pinafore tied round her ample waist and she wore thick round glasses. I remember them both sitting down at the large wooden table in the sitting room, newspapers spread out before them. They proceeded to select the horses they fancied to win that day.

This is where my Grandmother's brother, uncle Jack, who lived in the back-to-back houses opposite Franklin Street came in. He would call for the bets to take them down to the bookies. Now I know why uncle Jack with his flat cap and smoking a woodbine was always walking up and down – he was a bookies runner!

As I have said aunt Liza was a very down to earth person and if anyone needed a smack on the backside (using a much stronger word) she would say so. Hearing this word my brother and I would retreat into the backyard putting our hands over our mouths to stiffle our giggles.

If as kids we should be heard saying 'damn' or 'blimey' there was a quick shout, "Get in that kitchen and wash your mouth out". A picture of the red carbolic soap flashed in front of my eyes. The threat of that made us very careful of what words we uttered!

Sweet Treats

Families didn't move very far away after marriage, several lived just a stones throw away, mainly on gran's side. Just below gran's house lived her brother Bill and her sister-in-law Nell, who owned the grocery and sweet shop. They had three daughters Daisy, Nancy and Sylvia as well as two sons Harry and Kenny. Sylvia was more my age which was quite handy, she would smuggle a couple of sweets out hidden in the pocket of her navy blue school knickers!

Gran and Grand-dad Wise with daughter Thurza, 1920.

On the outside wall of the shop was the YZ chewing gum machine. For every fourth coin you got one free, we hoped our half-penny was the lucky one.

The red Brooke Bond van came regularly to the shop, this meant Sylvia would be told "Quick, fetch your aunty Gert down, the Brooke Bond man has arrived!" Mum would whip off her pinafore before scurrying down to the shop. They must have

7

had a great time, an hour later mum would return home her face flushed and her eyes still wet from laughing. She would be greeted by "Where on earth have you been all this time?" "Oh just down aunt Nells" was mums reply.

Opposite grans house was "Keytes" sweet shop, whose windows were full of goodies, it was a childrens paradise, with black jack chews, candy cigarettes, chocolate tobacco strands that melted in your mouth. Gob stoppers that you sucked for ages, long lasting strips of toffee, lucky bags with an assortment of sweets plus a transfer to stick on the back of your hand, leaving a pretty picture. Liquorice root you sucked until it was soft and gooey. Pear drops and kali sherbert babs. Bubble gum to chew and see who could make the largest bubble, until it burst and stuck to your lips. The last one was not a favourite buy with our mothers. Small bars of milky way chocolate were a real treat and you could have four chocolate dates for tuppence, rather expensive but worth every bite!

Home Entertainment

Every house had one - a fly catcher suspended from the ceiling, near to the light. This you bought in a round container. On removing the lid you pulled a ring to reveal a strip of sticky brown substance. The flies being attracted to the light would get caught on the fly-catcher. I suppose looking back it wasn't a pretty site, but that was before fly sprays came on the market. Radio was our only means of hearing the news and listening to entertainments. "In Town Tonight" was a programme of celebrities. Comedy and songs from Gracie Fields, affectionately known as "Our Gracie". Elsie and Doris Waters, sisters playing Gert and Daisy in their charlady act. Their brother, Jack Warner, later on became famous for "Dixon of Dock Green". Also he featured in the film "The Blue Lamp".
Derek McCulloch was our "Uncle Mac" on children's hour. The Western Brothers were known as "The Two Cads" and were very funny in what they said about people.
Henry Hall and his dance band got your feet tapping. Charlie Kunz entertained us with his brilliant piano playing.
The boring part on radio was listening to the football and horse-racing results, when us kids had "gorra be seen and not heard!"
Games we played in the house were Ludo, Snakes and Ladders or having a donkey drawn on paper, being blind-folded and trying to pin his tail on in the right place!
Making things with newspaper, a boat with sail that floated on water until it sank, an aeroplane you tried to glide round the room without hitting grand-dad! A piece of paper folded as many times as you could and cutting bits out with scissors, when opened would reveal a pattern you had created. These games amused us for hours and didn't cost anything.

Foundry Road School

In 1931, at the age of five years old, I started going to Foundry Road School. There were no play schools or nursery places to go to before you reached school age.

Arriving there holding mum's hand tightly, we walked into the hall where Miss Standeven, the headmistress, was waiting to greet us. Calling out our names I reluctantly left mum's side to join the other children.

We were led into the classroom which was very bright with colourful pictures on the walls, also I noticed that in the corner were building bricks and wooden toys.

After breaktime we would have to put our heads down on the desk for a little rest. I can remember the smell of the polish wafting up my nose, even to this day that memory is still there. My most memorable time in the infants was May Day, where we danced around the Maypole. The girls were dressed in white frocks and had a white flowered headdress. We carried little baskets of petals, which we scattered as we danced around. A May Queen was chosen and we walked behind her until she reached her special chair. Then we either sat or stood on benches to have our photographs taken. This was in the year 1933.

When I moved into the juniors we had men teachers for the first time. A Mr Trelawe was the name I remember most. Maybe because he was rather strict, work was much harder and so was discipline!

On one occasion the juniors were putting on a play to be held in the hall. Being brought up to look after the pennies, I was reluctant to ask mum for the money to go and see the play.

When the play was on, a friend and I went up to the school to peep through the window. Unfortunately we were caught and had to stand in the hall every playtime for a week.

When mum heard about this she asked "Why didn't you ask for the money?" It was a case of a no-win situation.

Still deep down I thought I did save you the money mum!

May Day 1933.
That's me, very back row, 2nd from right.

Walking to Save the Pennies

It may seem from reading my book that my brother Gerald and myself had a reasonably good life in the 1920s - 1930s. With our parents sacrificing what maybe termed as luxuries, we did have a happy life. We appreciated their need to save money where possible, for when they got a house of their own.

Living with dad's family, as good as they were, was not an ideal way of starting married life. Another urgent need for money to be saved, was for mum to pay a visit to her hometown of Swanage in Dorset.

So the old saying "Save the pennies and the pounds will look after themselves" was certainly true. It was a good lesson for my brother and myself in our future years.

The places mum and dad took us to were mainly within walking distance. A walk up the cut (canal) watching the barges full of coal being pulled along by large horses.

A walk up the "Wicket" origin apparently unknown, but could be a shortened version for "Smethwick". This walk would lead you to Thimble Mill Lane and the market.

Edgbaston reservoir was just twenty minutes walk away, so quite handy to spend a few hours fishing there.

Where we did have to rely on transport to get to other places, was on outings to Happy Valley in Yardley Wood, a day spent at the Lickeys and a 32 Tram ride for a day in town.

Shopping Days

My father worked at Johnny Wrights the gas stove maker in Thimble Mill Lane, Aston.

I remember one winter's day mum made a special stew for dad and put it in a basin covered with a teacloth and tied with string. We set off my brother and I toddling beside mum, it seemed a long walk to dad's factory. We must have gone some of the way by tram or bus, but all I can remember was the long - long walk!!

On Saturday afternoons we would all go to the market up Cape Hill, Smethwick. First we went up the "Green" taking a short cut down Heath Street, across Tudor Street leading into Winson Street, then up to Dudley Road. Walking up Cape Hill the Grove cinema was on our right, across the other side on our left was Mitchells and Butlers brewery. The smell of the hops wafting up our noses seemed to linger for ages.

The market would be bustling with shoppers anxious to obtain some bargains. The sellers trying to encourage the people with their special knock down offers! They would throw in some offal with the meat as an incentive to buy. Vegetables bagged up and sold off, speckled fruit given away. There was a great furore with the shoppers haggling for bargains. Shopping completed we would be treated to a windmill or a dicky bird on a stick which when swung round, made a twittering noise keeping us quiet on our long journey home.

One of mum's favourite places for shopping was the "Flat", Hockley. The greengrocers abounded with fruit and vegetables. Hanging up were rabbits galore. Mum would choose the one she wanted and the man then skinned it for her. This would make a good dinner with home-made sage and onion stuffing, or boiled with plenty of vegetables and some pork bones to enhance the flavour. It is hard to believe that my brother and I fought over who got the head.

Things you don't see these days is a cod's head on a fishmonger's slab. Mum would buy one, boil it, then scrape the flesh off the bones, mix with mashed potatoes turning it into a pie.

With the men's wages being so low, most women had to be thrifty with their money. Dad usually bought some pieces of leather and nails to mend our shoes when they needed repairing.

The shopping area up Cape Hill.
By kind permission of Four Seasons.

Home Grown Vegetables

Occasionally we spent the day at grand-dad's allotment, this was on the opposite side to Lightwoods Park before the new estate was built. Arriving at the gates and walking along the pathway, we knew when we were approaching his plot. The aroma of the "gillies" wafted towards us, their sweet scent filling the air. In his shed a paraffin stove to boil a kettle of water for a cup of tea. Gerald and I were delegated the job of spraying the crops with the water pumps. This was fatal in the hands of us kids who delighted in spraying each other as well. Suddenly a shout from grand-dad "Ay, what are yow two doing!" stopped us in our tracks.

Home grown vegetable marrow achievement.
Judge by the box of Englands Glory matches in front.

In the fruit season there would be gooseberries, raspberries, blackcurrants and rhubarb to pick. When we got home any flowers we had over were put into bunches, sticks of rhubarb into bundles and put into separate galvanized buckets and sold at the front doorstep, not before retrieving a couple of sticks to dip in a cup of sugar!

On Sundays the family read the days newspapers but we were not allowed to see the News of the World! Which perplexed us somewhat. Although we had heard there were naughty people about, in fact we were warned not to speak to strangers or take sweets off them. I took this warning to heart when we were shopping in Handsworth market on Soho Road. Mum and dad were busily walking around when a man stopped to have a conversation with them. As the man left he shoved a sweet in my hand. When we got outside I threw the sweet into the gutter, well it could have been poisonous! I was taking no chances.

Our pleadings for a baby brother or sister were met with a definite NO. Even though being found in the yard with our hands together praying to Jesus to send a little baby – it didn't work.

Looking at the discarded pram in the corner of the yard, we cajoled dad into making a go-cart out of the wheels. The pram, no longer wanted, was dismantled, a plank of wood was retrieved from the shed, two shorter pieces of wood for the wheels back and front to be attached. A box fitted for the seat, rope leading from the front support to enable us to guide our homemade super go-cart racing machine.

Out on the street ready for the off, Gerald had first go because he was the youngest! I pushed the cart down the street having a few brushes with the gutter until we reached the passage just around the corner. I tried to push Gerald back but having knees grazed on the 'orse road' he reluctantly helped to pull the go-cart back up.

Then it was my turn, sitting in the seat adjusting my feet on the steering panel, Gerald gave me an almighty push that sent me downhill, the only way I could stop was using my shoes as brakes!

Well as we were novices there was no time to get more professional especially as the other kids were bringing out their go-carts.

A Trip to the Sea-side

The great day arrived when enough money was saved to enable mum to take us on the steam train to visit her beloved parents she had left behind in her home-town of Swanage, Dorset.

I was just three years old and Gerald eighteen months. On our first visit, being just a youngster, the memories are rather hazy. The country-side resembled a giant carpet of beautiful yellow primroses, their aromatic scent filling the air, this did leave a lasting impression with me.

This lovely picture of playing in the sands, mum with her cloche hat which was the fashion in the 1920s, makes a happy holiday photograph.

Our second visit to Swanage was in 1932. I was six years old and could appreciate mum's longing to see her parents. A monthly train ticket was purchased for our journey, unfortunately dad had to stay behind working.

We were very excited we were going to the sea-side on the steam train, even though the red seats were rough and made the backs of our legs sore. The rhythmic sound the wheels made going over the tracks "de-dum, de-dum, de-dum" had your head moving from side to side as if in a trance you started to go to sleep, when a sudden jolt woke you up. We used to look out of the windows until we were coming to a bridge then it was all systems go to pull the windows up before the smoke from the train got in.

Arriving at our destination and making for gran's cottage we could feel the fresh country air tingling our noses, quaint thatched cottages, small farms and green fields. It was a joy to wander down the lanes, wild flowers lining the pathway.

There was no running water in gran's house. A tap outside had to serve the three cottages and a toilet across the yard housed a boxed wooden seat, trails of ivy curled round the edge, the door was squeaky and had a rusty latch.

Next door to gran lived Mrs Crabb. She wore a pinafore with sacking tied round, a cap and smoked a pipe! Inside her small cottage stood a table covered with a real lace cloth, a large dresser with loads of willow pattern plates, around the mantel shelf above the fireplace was red velour material with tassels hanging down. The shelf was full of knick-knacks she had collected. It looked like a treasure trove, probably worth a fortune today.

Uncles Ted and Henry got up at four in the morning to shoot a couple of rabbits for gran to make a nice stew. They would also collect some fresh field mushrooms for our breakfast. They tasted delicious.

Mum took us on lovely walks through the fields until we reached the cliff tops. The lovely singing of the birds, the crying of the sea-gulls capturing the smell of the ozone from the sea. On a clear sunny day you could see the cliffs of the Isle of

Wight. Mum always took us on this walk before we had to leave Swanage to catch the train home to Birmingham.

Gerald and myself with mum's sister Joan,
outside the back of gran's lovely cottage in Swanage

Monday, Washing Day

In the middle of Wellington Street, there were three terraces of back-to back-houses. The women had to share the brewhouse to do their washing.

Our coal fired brick boiler was up the corner of the kitchen. This would be got going at 5.30 on a Monday morning. Getting up for school and walking into the kitchen was like entering a turkish bath, steam was everywhere. The large wooden rollers of the mangle ready in the yard for the water to be squeezed out of the clothes. The washing then hung out on the line to blow dry. Woe betide anyone who had a chimney fire on wash day. The women of all shapes and sizes would dash up the garden and gather their washing in, muttering a mouthful of words as the sooty atmosphere threatened to besmirch their whites.

When the chimney sweep man had to call, everything would be removed from the overmantel above the fire place. Sheets and newspapers would spread over furniture to protect them from the coat dust. We would be sent out to see if the brushes were sticking out of the chimney pots. The soot was collected and taken up the top of the garden and had to be left for three months before it could be used on the garden because of the acid in it.

Another visitor to the street was the man who came with his grinding machine to sharpen knives or scissors. We stood and watched as sparks flew as he operated the pedal with his foot to turn the wheel.

Large blocks of salt were delivered by horse and cart, these would be stored in a cupboard under the stairs. This would be frowned on in this day and age!

An unwelcome caller was a gypsy who was swathed in colourful scarfs, wearing clothes down to her ankles and a basket on her arm. "Buy some lucky heather lady?" We urged mum to have some in case she put a wicked spell on us!

Taken Out for the Day

On school holidays mum never missed an opportunity to take us out especially if it was a nice day. One of these outings would be Lightwoods Park, Bearwood. This meant a walk up the "Green" a shortened version of Winson Green Road, then across Dudley Road and up City Road passing George Dixons School and the lovely large houses where it was alleged the rich people lived. We would carry on walking until we reached the Kings Head, Bearwood.

On the opposite side was Lightwoods Park. On entering we came across an aviary full of singing birds. Mum would be in her element hearing the birds twittering away, reminding her of the countryside she had left behind in her hometown of Swanage, Dorset.

The bandstand in Lightwoods Park.
By kind permission of Jue Russell's Family.

After a short while we made for the paddling pool. We were soon playing in the water. A loving brother delighted at being able to kick sprays of water over me, or ducking my head underneath the water. My screams going unnoticed as mum relaxed on the bench with her fingers going ten to the dozen, busily knitting another jumper.

All too soon it was time to stop playing and have our sandwiches. Then to round off the day mum would take us through to Warley Woods. It was great fun chasing about in between the trees, playing "Catch me if you can", or collecting pine cones to fill our pockets with. Then it would be time to take the long trek home.

Another place we loved to go was the Edgbaston Reservoir up Icknield Port Road, our fishing net and jam jars at the ready to catch some tiddlers. Obviously we had to see who could catch the most. Anyway we wanted to impress our uncle Harry. He was a real fisherman who had won many prizes. We hoped he would think we were budding anglers.

Goings On in Wellington Street

On leaving the house to go out to play, our ears ringing with a shout of "Mind the horse road!" then dad's quick reminder "If the horses have left anything behind, see that yow's fust to get the bucket and shovel!

The large horse pulling the 'Davenports' cart with crates of their beer was a welcome sight. Grand-dad would have one of these. In the evening sitting in his large wooden chair, out would come his special glass and leaning over towards the fire, he plunged the poker into the burning embers. After a while he then retrieved the poker and put it in his glass of beer, causing loads of froth to bubble up. "It's my hot toddy, helps to keep the bugs away!" he explained with a twinkle in his eye.

My Grand-dad

Occasionally a horse and cart came round with a merry-go-round on the back. You paid over your money to be put upon the seat, the man turning the handle to make you go round. If there were only a couple of kids you had a longer ride.

What really made our day, was the 'Victoria' breadman coming around with his horse and cart. He would lift us up to sit by him and give us a ride to the top of the street. The lovely smell of the freshly baked bread tickling our taste buds. He sold very small cottage loaves that were a treat with lashing of butter on. The rag and bone man was enough to send kids running into their houses asking for any old clothes. One day I spied on his cart a little type theatre, when you turned the handle it would roll pictures round behind celophane. He said I could not have it. I ran back to mum and told her. Mum came out and asked "Why!" The man said "Mrs, they cost 2/11d each." Mum retorted "Oh no they don't, they are 1/6d up the road, give me back the clothes". I got my theatre!

Voting day was great fun, we would dress our bikes up in the appropriate colours then ride round the streets, missing out the opposing streets, we weren't that brave!

When the men came home from work, in the evening we would all congregate in the street. Uncle Harry got the big bass drum out, saucepan lids, cake tins, anything the kids could bang. On we marched singing.

> "Vote, vote, vote for Mr Smith-th,
> he will sure to win the day.
> We will get a salmon tin, and put old Jones-e in,
> And he won't come voting anymore."

What a pity with all the traffic on the roads, the children miss out on this great fun-day.

Silver Jubilee, 1935.

1935 was a memorable year. King George V and Queen Mary celebrated their Silver Jubilee.

Plans were made in the street for the big event. Costumes made out of crepe paper for the children, buntings strewn across the street and windows and doors decorated.

The great day arrived with everyone filled with excitement. Tables, chairs and benches lined the middle of the street. Mothers, grans and aunts busily putting the sandwiches, cakes and jellys out for our great feast.

Later when the tea party was finished, tables and chairs removed, people brought out wind-up gramaphones and a couple of pianos. Games were laid on for the children, dancing for everyone lasted well into the night. It was a day when all let their hair down and had a thoroughly good time.

During the 1930s electricity was being installed in Wellington Street. When grand-dad was approached he said, "I am not having any new fangled stuff in this house". Sitting back in his large wooden chair giving extra long puffs on his pipe. "So that's that!" he added. Eventually with family pressure he gave in. The Brummies were well known for their sayings, if you left the door open a shout could be heard of "Put the wood in the hole, was yow born in a barn?"

Heads would have to duck if a 'bob howler' (moth) was flying around, someone would be chasing it with a rolled up newspaper.

When our Jack won some money on the horses, the cry was "Well I'm blowed, I'll go to the foot of our stairs!" If someone had a good run of luck dad's favourite saying was "If he fell of the top of Lewis's, he'd fall into a new suit!"

The family Jubilee, 1935

Jubilee party in Wellington Street, 1935

Shopping Around The Green

The local shops I remember were the greengrocer on Foundry Road. He displayed his fruit so temptingly. The apples shone as they nestled in their green tissue paper, small blood oranges always juicy and sweet, Victoria plums larger than eggs and greengages otherwise known as egg-plums. We looked forward to the fruit season as mum would be making home-made jam. That meant a few plums would be going spare.

The drapery shop owned by a Mrs Bird, stocked everything for the needs of the housewife. Dress-making pins, collar studs for the mens loose collars, rolls of lace edging, cottons and silks. Apparently if you had a farthing change to come, she would give you a handful of pins instead.

'Willeys' was the electrical shop where we had to take the wireless accumulator to be charged. For this to be done we had to pay sixpence. It looked a queer contraption, an oblong shape with glass sides and contained fluid. I later learned that this was acid.

'Trickets', the newsagents on Winson Green Road, stocked the black twist tobacco that we had to get Grand-dad for his pipe. It was known that some men would even chew it!

Further along was the sweet shop which held a fascination for the kids with a penny to spend. An oblong box covered in cardboard with numbered holes, a layer of silver paper fastened underneath. You picked up the bodger and poked through the hole of your choice to reveal a small packet. When opened you would see what sweet you had or if lucky maybe a ring.

'Hyde's' the dairy ice-cream shop, where our aunts would treat us at week-ends. A double cone for them and a cone cup of ice-cream for my brother and me. It tasted the best in the world.

Our favourite shop had got to be the faggot and peas shop just around the corner from Wellington Street, in Foundry Road. Carrying the basins ready to be filled, the aroma drifting towards us, mouths watering until we got home. It was the best take-away anyone could wish to have.

Winter Troubles

The really snowy winters of my younger days brings memories of looking through the bedroom window to see icicles thick as candles, hanging down from the guttering their droplets onto the window sill, leaving pretty shapes as they froze hard.

After school we were out making slides, having great fun until a lady, Mrs Warwick she was, came out and threw loads of salt melting our slide. We were rather angry and we didn't ask her to be blessed in our prayers that night!

Winter meant dark nights, going to the lavatory across two yards was frightening. The light from a paraffin lamp made eerie shadows on the painted walls. Even a small spider scurrying around looked as large as a tarantula! Hanging on a piece of string from a nail were squares of newspaper. Some were pinkish colour out of Saturday's Sports Argus.

In the shed hung the large tin bath which was brought in every Friday. Buckets of waterwere boiled on the black gas stove ready to add to the cold water in the bath. It was sheer bliss having a bath in front of the coal fire. Although we didn't think of the hard work involved in the emptying of the bath afterwards.

We had two dogs in the house, a beautiful Irish Red Setter with her coat of hair so shiny and silky. She was regularly groomed by my aunt Thurza who owned her and we had a small brown mongrel named 'pup'. She was adorable and very faithful, she loved having us kids around.

At the top of the garden we kept two rabbits and it was our job to clean them out and put new straw in. I remember one particular time when the rabbits were out of their hutch running about the garden. We had to reassure our parents that we had locked their door. However, all was soon to be revealed. Mum came in from the garden holding a boy by the scruff of his neck. "Here is the culprit who is letting the rabbits out!" I gasped when I recognised him from our school. He looked at me rather sheepishly and mum took him round to his house where his mother made him promise not to do it again.

Family Trauma

If anyone was feeling under the weather it brought forth the following comment, "What you need is a good dose of salts!" Funnily enough it seemed to cure most ills, maybe because it was cheaper than going to the doctors. Unfortunately the salts cure didn't work for dad. He was taken very poorly. We could sense the trauma in the family. He required the district nurse to call in daily. With cold water in the jug and the wash basin ready on the marble wash stand and a kettle of hot water taken upstairs when the nurse called. On one visit, mum with the nurse were in the bedroom, Gerald and I crept up the steep lino covered stairs holding onto the wall as there was no banister and sat on the top stair, our minds running riot. Suddenly the bedroom door opened, startled, we jumped up and fell to the bottom of the stairs. Mum and the nurse came rushing down worried in case there were two more casualties. Luckily, apart from a few bruises, we were unhurt. Mum reprimanded us for being on the stairs. We explained we were saying a prayer for daddy to get better. Mum gathered us up in her arms and a tear ran down her flushed cheek. The house was very sombre for a while until one day mum began singing "Hark at her singing with Charlie so ill" they cried. Mum turned to them with a look of serenity of her face, "He is going to get better, mark my words" she replied. Miraculously dad made a welcome recovery.

Dad was still on convalescence when he came up to Foundry Road School, he handed me an ice-cream cornet through the railings, unfortunately the bell went before I had eaten it. Well I wasn't going to waste it, so I put the cornet in my desk. Every so often I would take a lick. The teacher noticed this and asked

"Gloria, what are you doing keep opening your desk?" "Please miss, my dad bought me an ice-cream and the bell went before I could eat it" I replied. "Go into the empty classroom and finish it". Relief on my face, I trundled off and finished the ice-cream.

In the school all the classrooms led into the hall and at playtime we would all line up at the door and marched out one class at a time into the playground. Mr Griffiths was the headmaster in the juniors, he looked rather severe and we quaked in our shoes when he was around. One day Gerald's teacher came into the classroom and asked my why he wasn't at school. "He is bad miss" I replied. "I know" said his teacher, "But why isn't he at school?" I gulped, what was she saying about my brother?

We had to learn our times table in parrot fashion - one two is two - two twos are four. Our tables were so instilled in us, they went around in our heads as we tried to sleep. They say your school days are the best days of your life, well I enjoyed my days at Foundry Road School.

Gloria Wise, nine years old   *Gerald Wise, seven years old*
Happy days at Foundry Road School

All in a days work

Spring cleaning time was a hazard to us kids, we were glad to get out of the way - in fact were told to get out of the way!

"Go outside to play and mind the 'orse road and don't go down the so' pole" (soap-hole), the forbidden area.

Several of us would go on a treasure hunt around Victoria Street and Foundry Lane. Nettlefolds, Avery's and other factories were in this part of Smethwick. In the gutters were various pieces of metal, round discs, small curved and squiggly shapes. We didn't need a metal detector it was all there for us kids to gather up and put in the hessian bag we had retrieved from the garden shed. On arriving home we made for the back yard and tipped our findings out. Most would be discarded except for the round discs, these covered in silver paper looked like half-crown, which we used as pretend money when we played shops.

Getting back to the spring cleaning, the house would be cleaned from top to bottom. Curtains were fetched down and washed, blankets stripped from the beds and put in the washing tubs, feather beds shaken and turned over and small carpets flung over the line and beaten. My mum and aunts on their hands and knees scrubbing the lino floor covering. When all was finished newspapers were spread over the floors to make their cleaning efforts last a while longer.

Mum as a young girl worked in service to the gentry. She would arise 5.30am to enable her to arrive at her master and mistress house in time to serve breakfast. Her day consisted of cleaning, cooking and waiting on their needs. One day the lady she worked for came down to the kitchen to find mum making a cup of tea, "How dare a servant girl make a cup of tea, you will have what we have left in the teapot!" Mum was really put out by this remark. Half way through putting the cakes she had made onto the cake-stand, she slipped two into the front pocket of her apron. When she arrived home she gave one to her mother and she polished the other one off herself giving her great satisfaction.

There were many ladies of the houses she had worked for with a much kinder attitude towards their servants.

Happy Valley

As my life revolved around Winson Green, I never cease to be amazed how my parents found such an enchanting place as 'Happy Valley' in Yardley Wood. This necessitated a journey by bus which was a novelty and a luxury. Arriving there among the crowds who had come to this popular rendezvous, we walked along the tow-path of the canal. Hedgerows lined the one side with wild flowers caressing their green branches. Below a ditch ran at the edge, we were busy floating twigs in the stream when we became aware mum had stopped, she knelt down and picked some watercress and swilled if in the clear water before proceeding to eat it. My brother and I watched in horror, "You'll die" we cried as we clung to her coat, "don't eat it". Waving her hand in the air she replied, "I've eaten plenty of this in my life time."

Keeping a close eye on mum for a while, we started to relax and skipped along the tow-path occasionally throwing stones into the canal. This was so much better than the weekly walk up the local cut (canal).

We stopped to have a picnic mum had prepared for us. The fresh air had made us feel very ravenous and we devoured every morsel.

Taking a casual walk back to the bus terminus with just time to have an ice-cream from the bungalow in the village, before boarding the bus for our journey back home.

Friendship

It must have been a wrench for mum leaving her relations and friends in Dorset when she came to Birmingham to live. We were pleased when she met a lady named Mrs Rogers to be known by us kids as aunty Rogers. Their meeting took place after a morning's shopping at Smethwick market. The lady was laden with heavy bags so mum offered to help her to her house in Tudor Street, Winson Green. Their friendship took off and lasted a lifetime.

Aunty Roger's house was up a long entry leading into a small courtyard. The out-house attached to the house contained facilities for washing and cooking. Another door led into the living room which seemed cluttered up with her possessions. Hanging from the ceiling was a round bird cage with a beautiful yellow singing canary. The winding stairs leading to the bedroom and attic looked treacherous to climb, broad at one end and very narrow at the other.

On school holidays we would accompany mum to visit her for a few hours. Aunty Rogers was some years older than mum. She loved wearing jewellery and had several necklaces around her neck. One in particular had beautiful coloured round and oval beads set in a silver chain. Rings adorned her fingers and black lace-up boots peeped from under her skirt.

I sat in awe listening to her wonderful stories of her young days in the Victorian era, and her knowledge of everyday current affairs. Just one item sticks in my memory, her foretelling that a bag of sugar which was only pence would go up to four shillings! We thought this was most improbable, but the dear lady was right. I wonder if she is looking down from up above and saying "I told you so", in fact in the 1990s a bag of sugar cost a staggering 70p (14 shillings).

Recalling Times in 1930

There were many historical events in the 1930s that had a profound impact on me. The woman pilot Amy Johnson amazed me with her bravery. I savoured any news forthcoming from the wireless or seeing the 'Pathe News' at the picture house. Her gallant journey to Australia had me spellbound, a sense of relief flowed through me when she landed in that far distant land.

Amelia Erhardtt was another woman pilot I listened to intently on our accumulator run bakelite wireless. She had made a journey across the Atlantic Ocean, along with other flights. I was over-awed by their exploits which were captured in a book of famous women I had bought for me. Unfortunately, I haven't had their spirit of adventure to fly, my feet have never left the ground.

The opening of Sydney Harbour Bridge brought fantastic pictures of this great event. I was fortunate to receive a jig-saw depicting the harbour giving me great satisfaction fitting all the pieces together to reveal their famous achievement.

News of the Crystal Palace being burnt down was devasting, the glass was made at 'Chance Bros.' Smethwick, a local factory.

I took an interest in historic events that happened around the world especially when watching the news at the cinema, I felt a sense of being transported to these different areas.

Playing in the 'orse road was my adventure playground, a rope tied round the top of the lamp post enabled me to swing round, pulling my legs up I could dream I was flying. What better for getting rid of pent-up energy than whacking an old bicycle wheel with a stick up and down the street, making a terrible din especially when other kids joined in. We found this great exercise - to be honest exercise didn't come into it, we just enjoyed having a bicycle wheel race.

Some mothers, having finished their work, would sit on the steps having a natter while their kiddies played. A toddler about 18 months old would go over for a feed, his mum promptly putting him on her breast. A flat capped man passing by would utter "That's right missus, give him what's best for him." Gerald, on one occasion seeing this, ran into mum and was pulling on her apron, "Mummy, mummy come quick, a lady's got a dummy on her chest and the baby's licking it!" Mum told me that amusing story.

The Hanging, 1936

Winson Green Prison looked a very forbidding place especially when approached from Villiers Street, as it was directly opposite.

Winson Green Prison, April 1936.
Birmingham Post & Mail.

There had been four hangings throughout the 1930s. The one which had remained in my memory was the hanging in 1936. I was nearly ten years old and became more conscious of what it meant. Dorothea Nancy Waddington was sentenced on February 27th 1936 to die for the killing of Ada Baguley. She had been nursed by Nancy Waddington.

Uproar raged throughout the country at the death sentence. Letters were sent to the Prime Minister, but to no avail. The hanging was to take place on April 16th 1936.

All the streets leading to the prison were cordoned off. A crowd of two thousand were kept well away. It was only when the notice was put on the prison gates that the people were allowed through, and were then able to read that the hanging had taken place.

She was the first and last women to be executed this century at Winson Green Prison. My friends and I went up to read the notice, then slowly made our way home.

Memories of the old Bull Ring

I am filled with nostalgia remembering the buildings of our great city. Lewis's, a wonderful building with the Minories separating the two parts. Walking through the store with mum, she would make a bee-line for the hat department. Knowing she would be some time, I sat down on the edge of a display stand and watched her trying on various hats. A cloche hat which was close fitting, then a wide floppy brimmed hat, the sides moving as she glanced side to side in the mirror. Turning to look at me with a smile on her face, followed by a wistful look of, if only I could afford this.

Normally after looking around the store, we would venture up onto the roof garden. You could see for miles over the tops of the buildings.

Looking back to the 1930s, when times were hard, the men worked long hours for little money, yet the town was bustled with people. Great stores like Greys, the Co-op, the Times Furnishing building stood out so magnificently. On the way down the Bull Ring, on our right was Peacocks with their uneven floor boards, counters full of clothes at bargain prices. The old Market Hall, sadly no longer there, remembered for the fishmonger's stall, their slabs full of fish of every description. Kippers, herrings, cod and roe. Kippers were dad's favourite, bones and all consumed. The butchers with pigs trotters, tripe, sheeps heads, ox tail and offal all on show. Further down Woolworths the store that sold everything from dinky curlers to cooking utensils.

The sound of a woman's voice shouting "Andy carrier", she was unique in the Bull Ring. The newspaper man's call "Spatch 'n' Mail". Continuing on down till we came to the last shop which was Ellis's the drapers. Mum would go in there and rummage through the piles of material, hoping to find enough to make a dress for me, and maybe a pinafore for herself. Around the corner into Edgbaston Street, was the faggot and peas shop. The aroma wafting towards us beckoning you inside. Sitting down at the small wooden tables we sampled their food. We felt so glad we didn't resist the temptation.

The other shops fondly recalled was the Kardomah, the aroma of roasted coffee beans filling the air, Kunzles window full of delicious chocolate cakes. Bywaters in Bull Street, surely their sausages were the best in town. The Beehive in Albert Street a store for a casual walk round. Lyons cafe in New Street for a quick cup of tea before catching the number 32 tram back home in Winson Green.

A Crust of Bread

The mums had to eke out their money as best as they could. One of the frequent sayings was "What you never have, you never miss". Our fill ups during the day would be a slice of bread off a crusty cottage loaf, spread with pure lard and a pinch of salt, or beef dripping on a piece of bread toasted by the fire. A pikelet or muffin toasted on a Sunday tea-time was the norm. The nearest we got to salmon was a jar of salmon paste. Any bread left over was made into a delicious bread pudding with sultanas and mixed spices.

The main meals would consist of dishes made from rabbit, boiling fowl, breast of lamb or brisket of beef with plenty of vegetables and sumptuous gravy, mopped up with a chunk of bread. Pearl barley, lentils and dumplings added to a stew bubbling away in a saucepan made a substantial meal. The women in those days knew how to make a little go a long way. Dad kept some chickens in a big pen up to the garden, so we did manage to have a few fresh eggs. He used to boil their feed in a bucket on the stove. He had a special name for it which I can't remember. I'm just glad it wasn't for us!

One day dad killed one of the chickens and left it on top of the pen. The lady next door saw it move and shouted "Charlie the chicken is moving" "Ah, he's dead but he won't lie down" said dad in his usual sense of humour. It is not unusual for their muscles to jump even after being killed.

The Black Range

There would be no fire to get up to on Friday mornings. This was black leading day with 'Zebra' polish. The grate would be polished until it shone, hearth scrubbed, the enamel decorated hearth plate washed and replaced in front of the grate. An ornate brass and wooden fender put in position around the fireguard.

Soft brown soap scooped out of a tin, ready for scrubbing the quarry tiles. Jeyes fluid was used to clean out the suff (drain). Buckets of the same disinfectant was thrown over the yard then brushed vigorously with the hard broom. Last of all the entry and pavement would be given the same treatment. The doorstep cleaned using a grey-like pumice stone. Arriving home from school, everywhere looked nice and clean and smelt sweet.

Gran had a lot of remedies to combat illnesses. Goose fat that had been stored since Christmas plastered on your chest for a bad cough, said to prevent you catching a chill. Brown paper was added to stop the grease spoiling your clothes. Senna pods soaked in water over night, a spoonful good for the system. Friday night ritual of syrup of figs. A walk round the gas works to clear a cold, or down a newly tarred road which was definitely more pleasant. A cold key dropped down the back of your neck to stop hiccups. The washing blue bag dabbed on a wasp sting relieves pain. Chew you food 32 times, that's how many teeth you have! And the ultimate favourite saying "Sing at your meals trouble at your heels".

When the Doctor had to call

The front door of the house leading into the parlour, was only opened for important visitors, such as when we needed Doctor O'Dowd to call. He would arrive on his bike which he left against the house. In his hand he carried a large black bag with a strong brass fastener. We had to make ourselves scarce while he seen to the person who was ill.

His surgery was on the corner of Handsworth New Road, on the opposite side was the chemist's Bannister and Thatcher. Their shelves full of all kinds of medicine and pills. Beechams Pills, Bile beans, senna pods, camphorated oil to use when you had a cold. He stocked many remedies to help people combat everyday needs. It was quite expensive in those days for calling on doctors, the chemist's were much needed.

Winson Green Road was always referred to as the 'Green'. One day going up the 'Green' with my friends, we looked across the canal bridge to the back of the asylum. We noticed the nurses wheel the patients in their beds out onto the balcony. We thought we would be kind and wave to them. Unfortunately they got excited and started jumping up and down. The nurses rushed out and got them back inside. Our good deed had gone wrong, we felt terrible.

We decided to go window shopping, the first shop we stopped at was the clothes shop. Ladies corsets with steel bones and laced right up the front and with suspenders. We wondered how our mums managed to work with these on. Lisle stockings, way before nylons came on the scene. Bloomers with elastic round the legs. Interlock cream vests with ribbon threaded through the neck opening. Wrap around pinafores tied at the front and then at the back, all the women wore them. I suppose it was to keep their frocks clean. They just had to whip their pinnies off and they were ready for shopping.

Next we came to the grocers which seemed to be cluttered up with tins of fruit, golden syrup, black treacle. Blocks of butter which he used wooden butter pats to shape to the weight you wanted. There was a box with a piece of metal with holes in and a light underneath. He would stand eggs up in the holes, switch in a light and if the eggs were cloudy he discarded them. On the counter he kept a dish of cracked eggs he sold off cheap. Having enough of window shopping we made our way home just stopping to buy a sherbet dab.

A Tram Ride to Lickey Hills

Lickey Hills had to be one of our best days out. Dad and mum would take us on the 32 tram to town, then making our way over to Navigation Street to join the queues waiting for the tram to the Lickeys.

When the tram arrived my brother and I made for the upstairs balcony, there were no windows just railings around. The seats were made of wooden lathes. As the tram gathered momentum along the track, wind blowing in our faces, our bottoms slid on the slippery, shiny seats. It was very invigorating. The tram going slowly up the gradients and then with great speed down the other side until we reached our destination.

Once at the Lickeys walking up the long winding pathway towards the woods, pieces of twigs crunching under the thick leather soles of my shoes dad had repaired for me. Gathering and filling our pockets with pine cones and acorns. The usual game of hide-and-seek in the woods with mum and dad joining in. Suddenly there was a sound disturbing the still air, "cuckoo - cuckoo" this was dad giving a clue to his where-abouts. I hope other visitors weren't fooled by his bird call.

Reaching the top of the hill we felt we were on top of the world, the view for miles stretched before us. Mum spread the blanket on the ground and rummaged in her basket retrieving the home-made sandwiches and fairy cakes and a flask of tea to swill it down.

Full up and satisfied, we sat there a while taking in the beauty of the scenery, the fresh air so pure and sweet tickled our noses. The stress lines on dad's face caused by the long working hours gently eased. Mum enjoying the quietness of sitting there with just her family by her.

All too soon time to make our way back, passing the little waterfalls Gerald and I threw our lollipop sticks in, we raced them downstream, invariably one would get stuck, it was always the other ones that got stuck. A last treat of an ice-cream before joining the queue at the terminus for the tram journey home.

Behind Closed Doors

We found it rather chilling watching dad shave using an open cut razor. He would sharpen the blade on a strop which was fastened over a hook on the wall. Holding the side of his face he deftly brought the blade across his growth of stubble. Invariably he would cut himself and utter the cry "Ay, I've fetched blood!" This then would be covered with a small piece of newspaper.

There was no tooth brush or tooth paste, we had to improvise by cleaning our teeth with rubbing our finger into soot and salt! Any cuts we received whilst playing were cleaned up and wrapped up with rags.

My dad in his younger days

A typical pantry shelf contained the following items, a packet of shredded suet, dried peas with a bi-carb tablet, a bottle of camp coffee with chicory, a tea-caddy for loose tea, ovaltine, packets of flavoured jellies, pearl barley, lentils, dried fruit and nutmegs. Fresh mint and parsley was gathered from the garden. Thyme and sage tied up and hung in the lobby to use when dried.

We had no fridges in those days, a make do meat safe

made out of wood and covered with a fine mesh to make sure no house flies got on any left overs such as polony, black pudding or luncheon meat.

Although the family were more or less teetotal, they did have a hobby of making home-made wine. Bottles of parsnip wine, dandelion wine and elderberry wine was stored in the lobby under the stairs. Dad, who didn't frequent pubs, liked the occasional bottle of cider.

Ironing was done on the wooden kitchen table, using the flat iron heated on the gas and given a quick rub on the soap. The men were particular about their starched loose collars, they had to be just right. I heard many a strong word muttered under their breath trying to fit their collar studs in.

Aunty May had lovely long hair reaching down to her waist. This she would make into plaits, winding them up into a bun each side of her head and held in place with numerous hair pins. On going out she wore long leather gaiters with buttons all down the sides. Using a button hook she had the tedious job of pulling the buttons through the loops. These were very fashionable with the ladies in the 1920s.

1920s portrait of my aunty May

Playing our Favourite Games

The many games we played in the street brings back happy memories. Hide-and-seek was a favourite, there were so many alleyways and entries you could hide in. "Come out, come out, where ever you are the cats coming to find you". Hoping if you were near them, they would dart out and try to move somewhere else.

Tip cat was challenging. It was a piece of wood sharpened at each end with a bat to hit it with. On striking the tipped end, the first to get it over the chalked line was the winner.

Whip and top had us all going to see who could keep the top spinning the longest. We tried to compete with each other decorating the tops with different coloured paper.

The boys playing football in the street had the girls as look-outs for the 'Copper' coming round the corner. The boys scarpered up the alleyways when we all shouted that the burly Copper was on his way!

Sometime during the year we would have 'Curio' shops. Toys, books, games or cigarette cards we no longer wanted would be laid on the pavement in front of your house. Then you sat down beside them singing "Who'll come and buy my curios?" Hoping to make a sale then you could go and buy off the other children. Doing this selling, I suppose you could say we started the first out-door market in Wellington Street.

Another exciting time we enjoyed, was on a special occasion, an illuminated tram would arrive at the terminus. All the kids with their mums and dads, stood around mesmerised at this colourful event. How sad at the going of the trams, this wonderful time has now gone.

The Uplands Smethwick

Winson Green was a maze of streets. Mum and dad knew all the short cuts to save on tram and bus fare. As children we must have walked miles, this came in handy however when I became the proud owner of a bike known as a sit up and beg bike. The saddle was very close to the handle bars with a curved frame as opposed to the straight bar for the boys.

On one of our expeditions with my biking friends, we made our way down Wellington Street, then Victoria Street towards Windmill Lane, Smethwick, making a decision we would go to the Uplands Cemetery. What gave us this idea, I haven't a clue! On arriving there we walked around looking at the grave stones, reading their epitaphs when we became aware a lot of the graves had no flowers. Against the walls we noticed large white daisies growing wild. We went over and picked some, putting them in the empty vases. Feeling better for having done this, we made the long journey home.

My friends and I decided to join the Temperance Hall which was opposite Black Patch Park. The only thing I can recall happening there is we all had to stand in a circle and solemnly promise "I will not smoke, I will not swear, I will not drink". The last promise was easy after supping Gran's beer out of her jug in the entry!

(A photograph of Uplands Church appears on page 59)

Going to see Father Christmas

Christmas was always a great occasion to look forward to. We would be full of excitement when mum and dad said they were taking us to see Father Christmas in town.

This would mean a ride on the 32 tram to the terminus in Edmund Street. On arrival we would go through Eden Place, where a man who unfortunately had no legs, would be sitting on a wooden platform. Spread out in front of him were coloured chalks, which he used to draw pictures on the slabs. People gave money to him which they put in his cap.

Walking down Colmore Row making for the Great Western Arcade, we were thrilled to see all the Christmas lights and trimmings. Looking up to the balcony there was Father Christmas waving to us. We waved back to him, before going on to Henrys in Martineau Street. This was a favourite store for many people, they had bargains to suit most peoples pockets.

However, we were here to meet Father Christmas, down the broad wooden steps into the basement. He would be sitting with one sack for the girls and one for the boys. We told him what we wanted, and with his usual smile he said he would do his best.

Another yearly event we looked forward to was Pat Collins Fair. This was held on a piece of ground the other side of the railway bridge down Handsworth New Road. The sound of the fairground music built up our excitement. Large colourful horses going up and down as they went round. The ghost train cobweb was really eerie, when cobweb like strands tickled your face and skeletons peered at you in dimmed lights, turning our knuckles white as we gripped the rail.

We were glad when it came to the end of the ride. Then it was over to the coconut shy, where dad was in his element at the challenge of knocking the coconuts down off their stands with the wooden balls. He always came away with a couple of coconuts and a smile on his face.

A toffee apple bought for us would finish our night out. When we arrived home dad would pierce the top of the coconut for my brother and me to drink the milk. It was a job to get to sleep with the fairground music still ringing in our ears and thoughts of the ghostly ghost train!

The road trodden by many shoppers,
High Street, Smethwick.
By kind permission of Four Seasons.

Playtime

Christmas time was the highlight of the year, the expectancy of having new toys to play with filled us with delight. We had to be on our best behaviour as the great day drew nearer. On our shopping trips up Cape Hill we observed the toy shop windows stocked with new inventions. Our faces pressed against the cold glass of the window, Gerald was mesmerised, his eyes firmly fixed on an aeroplane with lights that really worked. I fell in love with a dolls house full of furniture which had a garage. We knew exactly what to wish for when the ritual on Christmas Eve arrived. Kneeling down a paper bag was put on the fire and we made a wish. Oh! how we wished! The paper bag floated up the chimney to Father Christmas, this was a good sign that our wishes would be granted.

After a rather restless night, on waking we crept on to the landing, and as if by magic Gerald's up to date plane was there, and so was the dolls house for me. A bright new penny, apple, orange and nuts were in our stocking. On the Christmas tree were little pink and white sugared pigs, cute little sugared bird cages and chocolate cigars covered with silver paper.

The aroma from the goose cooking for our dinner filled the air along with the Christmas pudding laced with stout boiling on the stove. Several 'joeys' silver thru-penny bits were added to the puddings. We hoped we would get one in our slice!

At tea-time the luxury of a real tin of red salmon, what a change from a jar of salmon and shrimp paste! We savoured each bite we took of the mouth-watering salmon sandwiches.

On the night we would have a good old sing-song around the 'joanna'. I was very fortunate to be blessed with the gift of playing the piano by ear. Requests for popular songs from the

wireless flowed in: Bye, Bye Blackbird – You made me Love You – Daisy-Daisy –You may not be an Angel – In the shade of the Old Apple Tree – Two Lovely Black Eyes.
A rousing 'Pack up your troubles in your old kit-bag' had Grand-dad going, with a twinkle in his eye and a cushion hung over his shoulder, he strutted round the room doing his stuff! 'Knees up Mother Brown', rounded off the night that must have rocked the foundations!

My World

Memories of Wellington Street include the railway bridge spanning across the street. Steam trains passed over frequently on their way to the station in the City, the train driver leaning out to wave to the kiddies playing in the street below.

Just around the corner from under the bridge, was the 'Soap Hole'. This was a very dark and dingy area, we were forbidden to play there. Apparently before 1930 the other side of this particular bridge was a factory making soap, hence the name soap-hole. I can hear dad's voice now saying "Don't you go playing down the 'So'pole!"

Opposite was the 32 tram terminus, the tram driver would go to the Bundy clock, put his key in and record the time of his arrival. On withdrawing the key we would hold out our hands for him to stamp the blue number on us. We would pretend we had a tattoo!

On the corner of Victoria Street and Wellington Street, stood the Railway Inn public house. It had red tiled sloping window ledges. A childhood dare was to see who could stay on the ledges the longest before sliding off.

Going up Wellington Street towards the Green, was the coal wharf, where we had to go to fetch half hundred weight of coal. Paying sixpence for the loan of the barrow, my brother and I wheeled the coal home. When the barrow was emptied, newspaper was put in the bottom, then we took it in turns to push each other back. Blowing our noses afterwards we were amazed how much coal dust we had breathed in.

There was also the Malt House, the men could just be seen through the murky windows, seeing to the sheafs of grain for the brewery.

The dispensary had gone and an outdoor was in its place. This is where we had to fetch Gran a jug of beer, which was quietly sampled in the entry by Gerald and myself

On the corner of Wellington Street and Winson Green Road was the 'Picture House'. Going there on a Saturday matinee to see Cowboys and Indian films which the boys loved. I liked the comdey films best, such as Harold Lloyd, Charlie Chaplin, Old Mother Riley and Shirley Temple. My favourite film has to be 'Rose Marie' with Nelson Eddy and Jeanette McDonald. He looked so handsome in his mountie uniform as he sang to her.

The Old Church, The Uplands, Smethwick.
By kind permission of Joe Russell's Family.

Moving On

As I have said at the start of my book, we lived with dad's relations in Wellington Street, Winson Green. Gran was not able to do much as she suffered with a back problem. She died at the age of 56 years in 1936. It was my first encounter with a bereavement. Mum did her best to console us.

Grand-dad worked in the iron foundry as a tube tester. He came home wich such tales about his friend Messy Causer. This is putting it politely! He got many a telling off by my aunt "Ay, not in front of the children." But he had such a twinkle in his eyes he made us laugh. Auntie May worked in the Jewellery Quarter in Regent Place, Hockley, assembling gold watch bracelets. I don't know if the premises were bombed in the war, as she went to work at 'Averys' who made the weighing machines. When she retired they presented her with a chiming clock. I am now the proud owner of this clock which will be kept in the family. Dad worked at Johnny Wrights in Thimble Mill Lane, Aston. He was a gas stove tester. At Christmas they gave wonderful parties for the children, with entertainments laid on. A special Christmas present for every child was given at the end. Uncle Harry, I do not know what his trade was, but his hobby was fishing. He did very well in competitions, winning many prizes. Aunt Thurza worked as an assembler in a local factory.

Mum and Dad were anxious for a home of their own. When an offer of a house in Kingstanding became available in the Spring of 1937, they were delighted. Moving there from Winson Green was like living in Siberia, it was so cold. Although we had a front garden and a bathroom, I missed the warm friendly atmosphere of Wellington Street where I had lived for the first ten and a half years of my life. Those happy days are locked in my heart.